AF255320

COCOA

At night as her mom was tucking her into bed,
Cocoa was thinking about her upcoming birthday and said,
"Mom, can I throw a party, next Saturday, please?
I promise to do it with grace and ease.

All my friends will be quiet when we meet,
and we'll mind our manners when we eat.
We're growing up and we know how to act,
just like adults with politeness and tact."

Cocoa said, "We'll be careful to keep the house neat,

but if we're messy or track in dirt on our feet,

by some chance, if something unexpected goes wrong...

my magic butterfly Boppie will help us along.

When the house is neat, everything's in its place,

and each object is positioned in the right space.

I promise that we'll do everything we can do,

to keep the house calm and orderly for you."

Dream
Big
You're Invited!
Where: Cocoa's Castle
MINDING YOUR MANNERS
IS SIMPLE TO DO,
JUST TREAT OTHERS
LIKE THEY SHOULD TREAT YOU.

So her mom said, "Yes! You may celebrate!"
Cocoa quickly mailed out invites for the party date.
And, in each invitation, she included in her note,
this very special, important quote:
Her note said…

"Minding your manners is simple to do,
Just treat others like they should treat you."

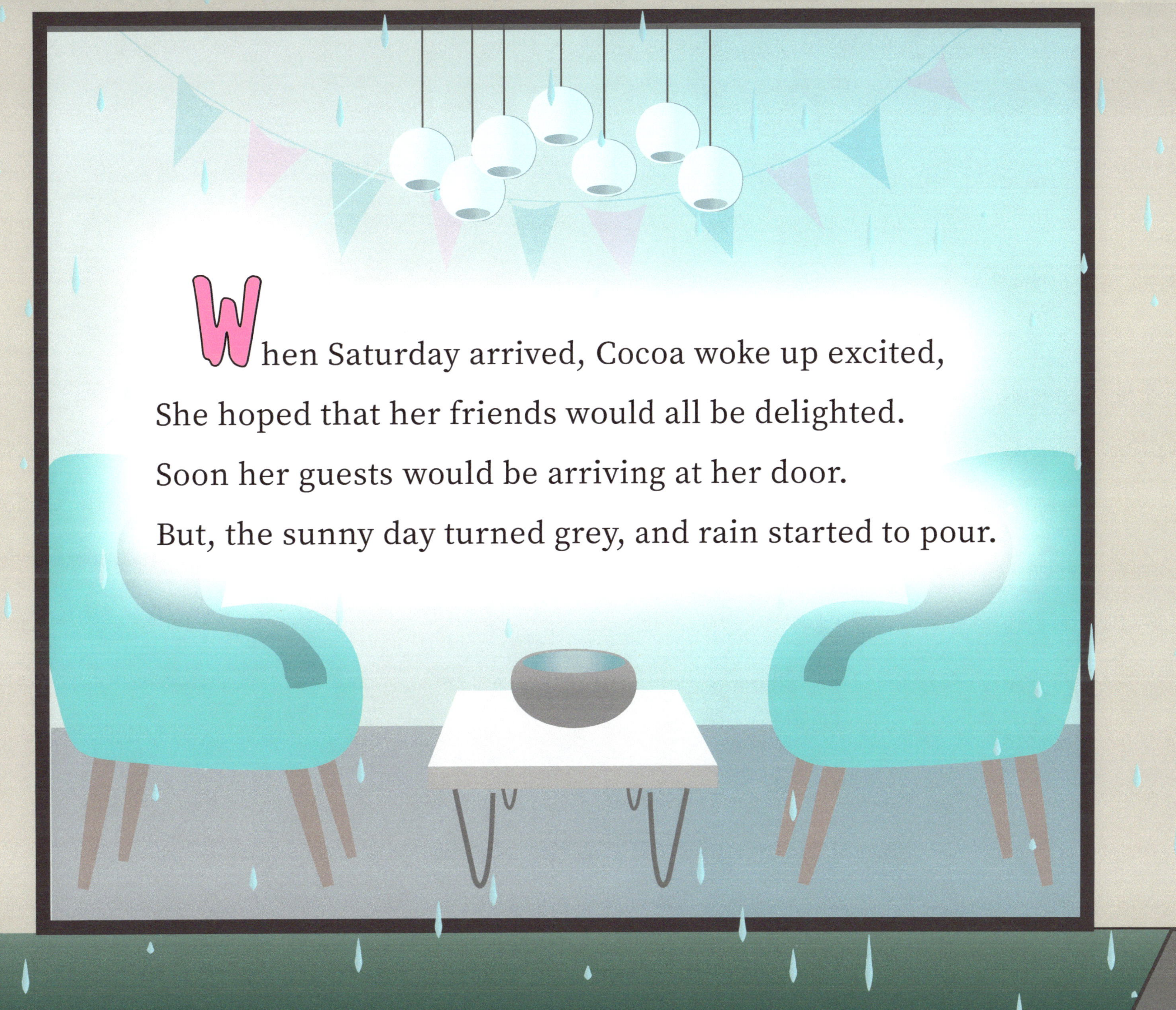
When Saturday arrived, Cocoa woke up excited,
She hoped that her friends would all be delighted.
Soon her guests would be arriving at her door.
But, the sunny day turned grey, and rain started to pour.

Cocoa's best friend, Paisley, was the first to show.

She was carrying a gift for Cocoa that had a soggy, limp bow.

Paisley said, "I'm here on time, but I'm soaking wet!"

Cocoa smiled, "Don't worry, we'll dry you off—don't fret!"

They were both busy talking so they didn't see

that Paisley was tramping in dirty footprints as plain as could be.

She had forgotten to wipe her boots...they were caked with crud.

The once-clean vestibule was soon filled with squishy, grassy mud!

"I'm so sorry!" said Paisley. "Where are my manners? What have I done?
Cleaning this big mess isn't going to be much fun!
I'm usually so mindful, but I forgot because we were talking…
I've left huge, muddy footprints everywhere I was walking!"

Cocoa was upset, but she tried hard to stay calm…
she knew that her mom would react with alarm.
Her mom had cleaned their whole house for this special day.
If she saw the dirty entrance, what could Cocoa say?

poof!

But, then, Cocoa heard a familiar tinkling sound...

She picked up and waved her magic wand around,

Her butterfly Boppie was helping them undo the mess.

Her confetti-colored sprinkles quickly calmed the stress.

Paisley found herself outside the door once more.

Cocoa said, "Now it's undone, so you can do it better than before!"

Paisley was astonished...there was a clean floor as she looked in.

She smiled and said, "This time I'll take off my boots before we begin!"

Then, Paisley said, "Wow! That was amazing. Let's put up a sign!"
Cocoa said, "I agree—that should keep everyone in line.
It should say, Please wipe your feet, then take off your shoes.
My mom would say—Good manners should always be what children choose."

So, they put the sign up right away and it was a good thing too,
Thanks to the notice, everyone knew what to do.
Lots of guests were arriving and barreling through the door!
Cocoa, Boppie, and Paisley had protected the clean floor.

Please wipe your feet, then take off your shoes.
Please wipe your feet, then take off your shoes.
BE KIND

hi my name is
Jackson
BE KIND
hi my name is
Easton
hi my name is
Cocoa
hi my name is
Addison
hi my name is
Paisley

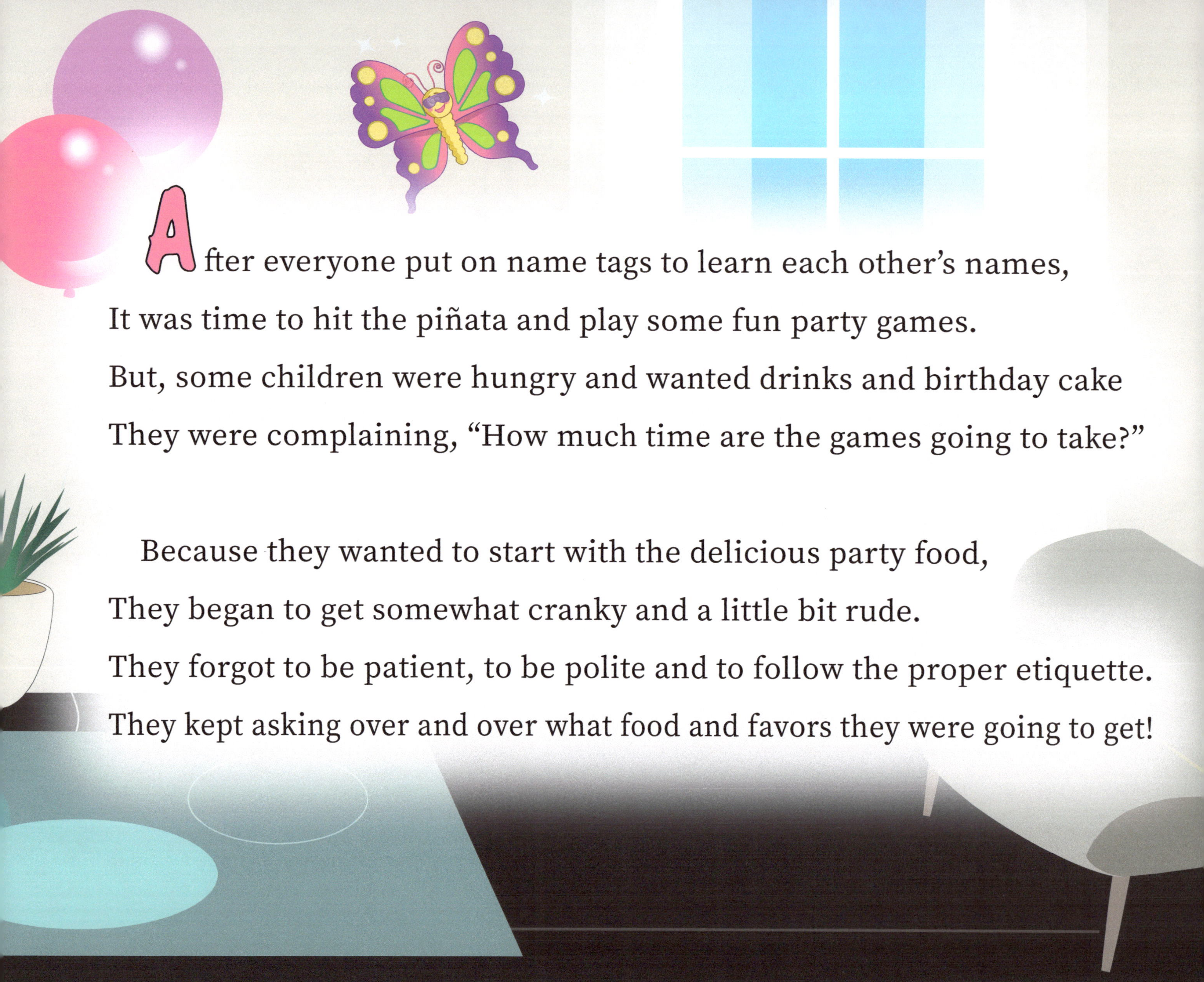

After everyone put on name tags to learn each other's names,

It was time to hit the piñata and play some fun party games.

But, some children were hungry and wanted drinks and birthday cake

They were complaining, "How much time are the games going to take?"

Because they wanted to start with the delicious party food,

They began to get somewhat cranky and a little bit rude.

They forgot to be patient, to be polite and to follow the proper etiquette.

They kept asking over and over what food and favors they were going to get!

So, Cocoa stood in front of the guests and spoke her mind.

"Please be patient! Say excuse me if your stomach growls, relax, and unwind!

My mom's getting all our food ready for the table.

She'll have the drinks, cake, and favors as quickly as she's able."

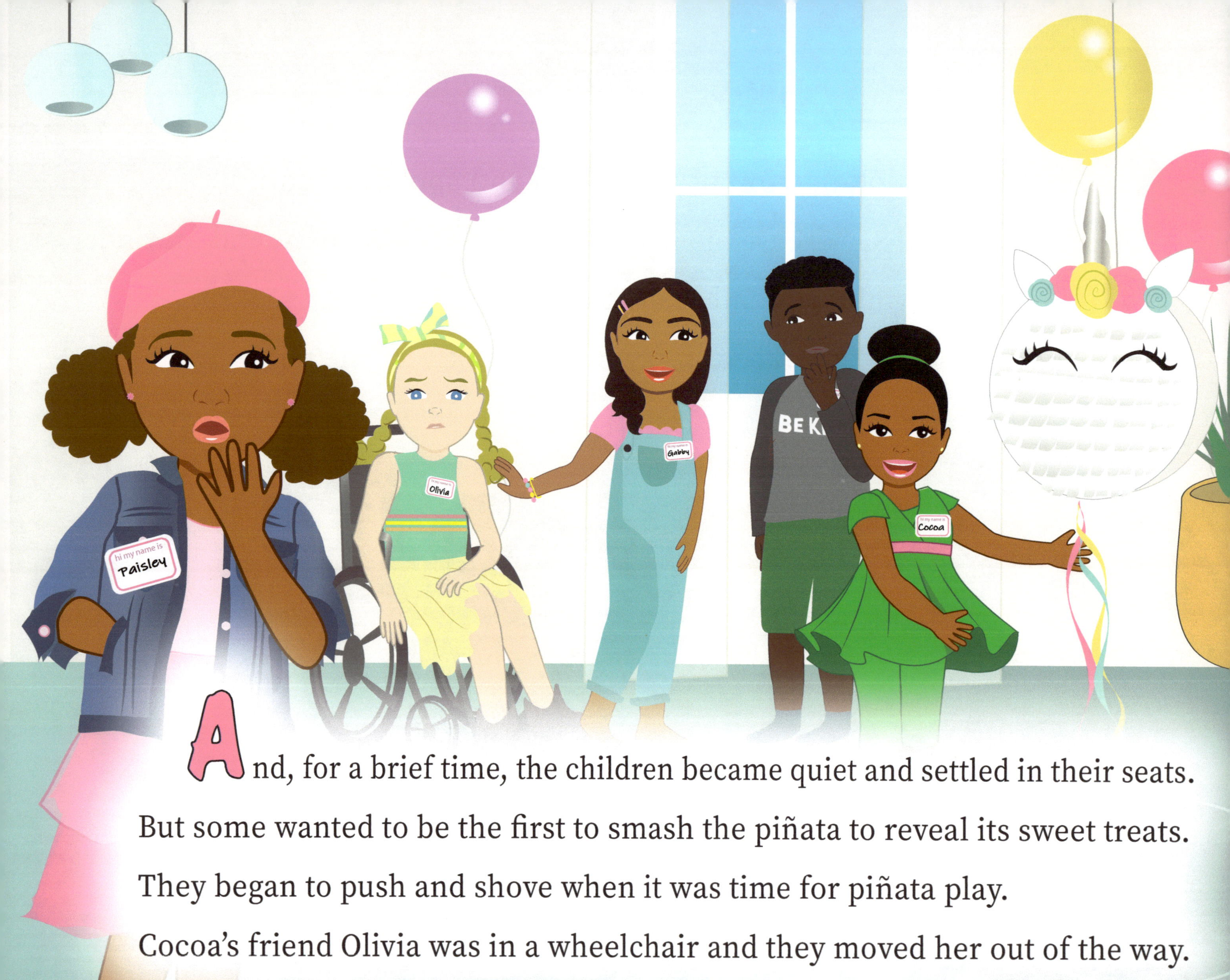

And, for a brief time, the children became quiet and settled in their seats.

But some wanted to be the first to smash the piñata to reveal its sweet treats.

They began to push and shove when it was time for piñata play.

Cocoa's friend Olivia was in a wheelchair and they moved her out of the way.

Cocoa's friends Payton and Jackson witnessed this impolite event.

They were waving their arms as they began to vent,

They came running up to Cocoa to tell her what they'd seen.

They thought the guests' lack of empathy was very mean.

Disappointed in her guests, Cocoa was becoming quite mad,

That's when she waved her magic wand to turn Anna's sad to glad,

It was time for Boppie to arrange a magical exchange.

And give her guests the chance to make the proper, polite change.

Payton
Jackson
BE KIND
Olivia
Paisley
Addison
Cocoa
Payton
Jackson
BE KIND
Olivia
hi my name is

hi my name is Jackson
BE KIND
hi my name is Gabby
hi my name is Payton
hi my name is Olivia
hi my name is Addison
hi my name is Cocoa

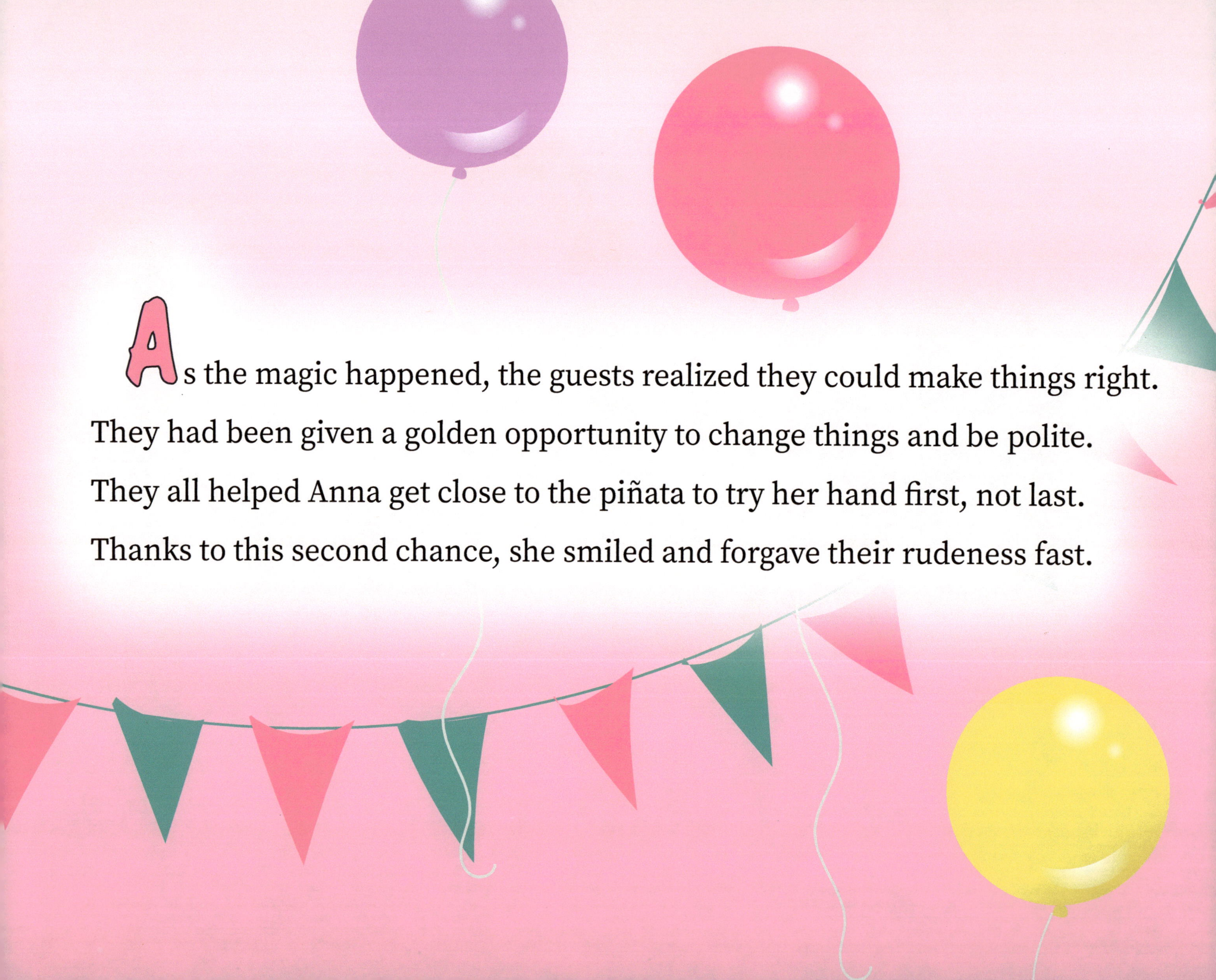

As the magic happened, the guests realized they could make things right.
They had been given a golden opportunity to change things and be polite.
They all helped Anna get close to the piñata to try her hand first, not last.
Thanks to this second chance, she smiled and forgave their rudeness fast.

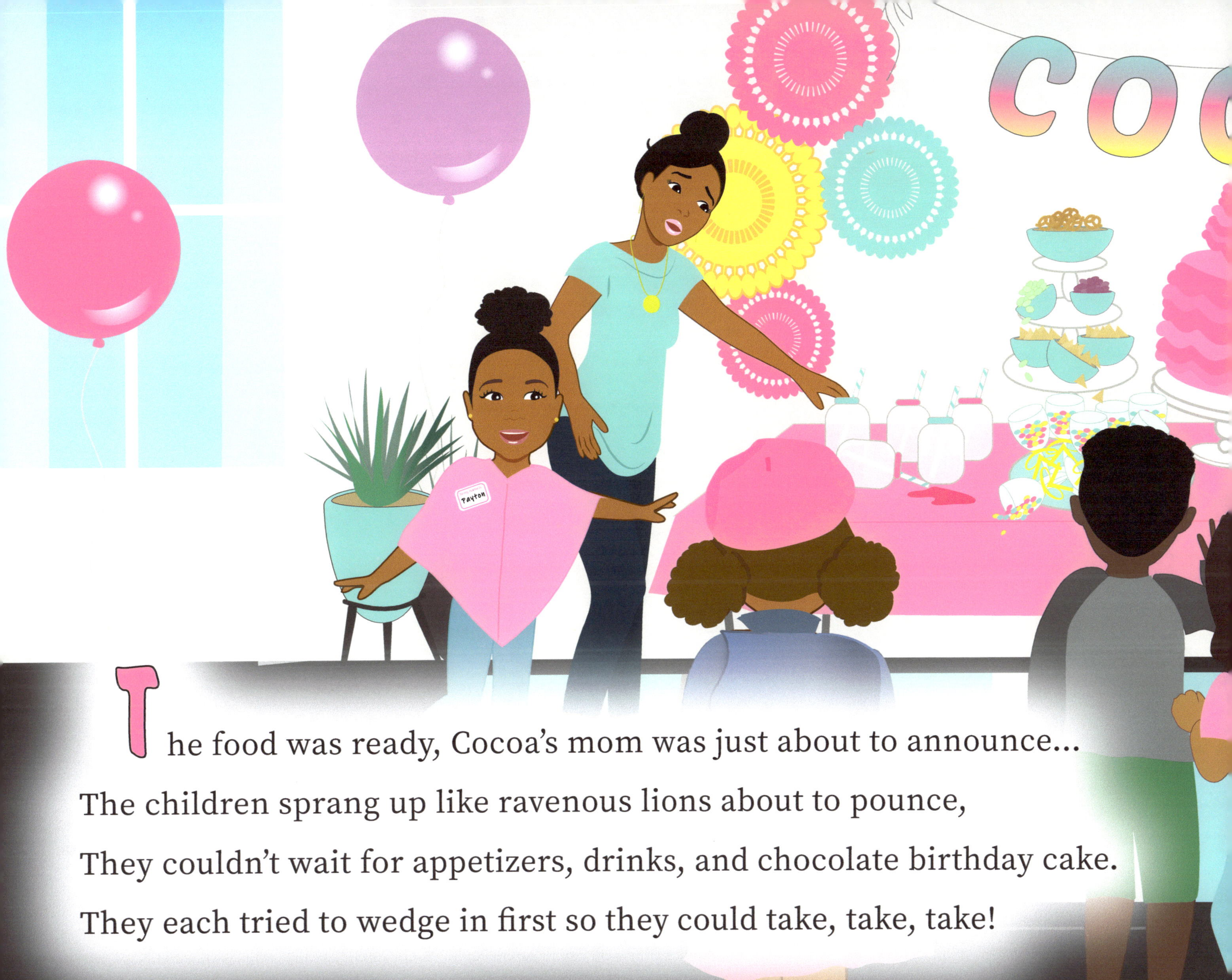

The food was ready, Cocoa's mom was just about to announce...

The children sprang up like ravenous lions about to pounce,

They couldn't wait for appetizers, drinks, and chocolate birthday cake.

They each tried to wedge in first so they could take, take, take!

Each of them was trying to cut in, instead of waiting for their turn,

"Oh, no!" cried Cocoa, "I thought by now they would all learn!"

As they bumped and shoved, the table started to shake.

Drinks were dropped and soon there was a tipping, toppling cake.

Everyone stood there in absolute horror—there was nothing to claim...

Their lack of politeness and good manners were certainly to blame.

The drinks were all spilled, the appetizers destroyed, and the cake was undone.

They all starting crying and whining and wailing, "No more fun! No more fun!

What have we done? We were rude and we didn't play nice.

Why didn't we listen and follow Cocoa's advice?

Minding your manners is simple to do,

Just treat others like they should treat you."

COCOA
Jackson
BE KIND
Cocoa
Addison
Olivia

Cocoa
Payton
Addison
Payton
Cocoa
Jackson
BE KIND

So, Cocoa put her hands on her hips and looked out at the enormous disaster…

"Instead of doing everything twice, starting all over might be faster!

Perhaps we should begin the entire day over with politeness in place."

And she knew she was right, when she saw a smile on each guest's face.

One last time, she waved her magic wand to change the view,

Cocoa's ill-fated birthday rewound from the beginning as if it were new,

And Boppie sprinkled confetti so they could begin at the start.

Everyone said please and thank you and it came from each heart.

Cocoa happily opened all her gifts before the day was done.

Things were easy and calm and it was all lots of fun.

They all played games, drank their drinks, and ate chocolate cake.

And when Cocoa's birthday was over, they had party favors to take...

So, if you're invited to a party, be sure to play nice,

Say please and thank you and remember Cocoa's advice...

"Minding your manners is simple to do,

Just treat others like they should treat you."

hi my name is Jackson
BE KIND
hi my name is Addison
hi my name is Payton
hi my name is Paisley
hi my name is Olivia
hi my name is Cocoa
Thank you!
Thank you!
Thank you!

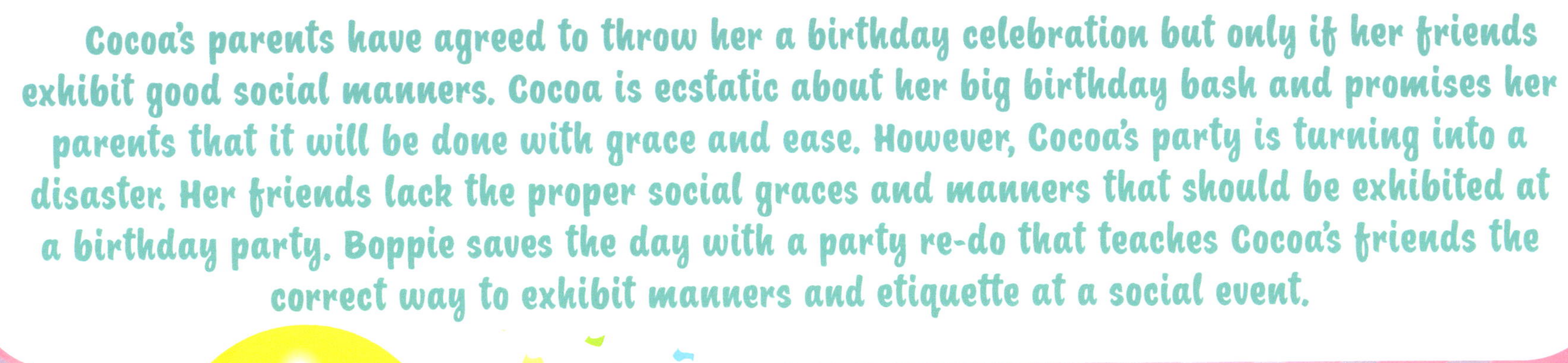

Cocoa's parents have agreed to throw her a birthday celebration but only if her friends exhibit good social manners. Cocoa is ecstatic about her big birthday bash and promises her parents that it will be done with grace and ease. However, Cocoa's party is turning into a disaster. Her friends lack the proper social graces and manners that should be exhibited at a birthday party. Boppie saves the day with a party re-do that teaches Cocoa's friends the correct way to exhibit manners and etiquette at a social event.

Author
Dr. Angelique S. Jackson

Illustrator
Heather Clevenger